Amazon WorkMail User Guide

A catalogue record for this book is available from the Hong Kong Public Libraries.

Published in Hong Kong by Samurai Media Limited.

Email: info@samuraimedia.org

ISBN 9789888407835

Contents

What Is Amazon WorkMail?

Amazon WorkMail is a managed email and calendaring service with strong security controls and support for existing desktop and mobile email clients. You can access their email, contacts, and calendars wherever you use Microsoft Outlook, your browser, or your iOS and Android mobile devices. You can integrate Amazon WorkMail with your existing corporate directory and control both the keys that encrypt your data and the location where your data is stored.

Amazon WorkMail works with all major mobile devices and operating systems that support the Exchange ActiveSync protocol, including the Apple iPad, Apple iPhone, Amazon Kindle Fire, Amazon Fire Phone, Android, Windows Phone, and BlackBerry 10.

You can access Amazon WorkMail from Microsoft Outlook on Windows. You must have a valid Microsoft Outlook license to use Microsoft Outlook with Amazon WorkMail, which offers native support for the following versions of Microsoft Outlook:

- Microsoft Outlook 2007, 2010, 2013, and 2016
- Microsoft Outlook 2010 and 2013 Click-to-Run
- Microsoft Outlook for Mac 2011
- Microsoft Outlook 2016 for Mac

Amazon WorkMail supports IMAP clients. For the required configuration, see Connect to Your IMAP Client Application. POP3 clients are not currently supported.

You can access Amazon WorkMail using the web application: https://*alias*.awsapps.com/mail.

Warning
To help protect your computer from malicious email attachments, we recommend that you install antivirus software.

Amazon WorkMail Pricing

With Amazon WorkMail, there are no upfront fees or commitments; you pay only for active user accounts. For more information, see Pricing.

Amazon WorkMail Limits

Amazon WorkMail has the following limits, which cannot be increased:

- The maximum size for a mailbox is 50 GB per user.
- The maximum size of an outgoing or incoming email message is 25 MB.
- The maximum number of aliases per user is 100.

Amazon WorkMail Languages

Amazon WorkMail is available in the following languages:

- English
- Russian
- French

Getting Started with Amazon WorkMail

Amazon WorkMail integrates with most popular email applications and devices so that you can synchronize your email, calendar, and contacts.

Topics

- Connect Microsoft Outlook to Your Amazon WorkMail Account
- Connect Your Mail App on Windows 10
- Connect Your Mail App on macOS
- Connect Your iOS Device
- Connect Your Android Device
- Manually Connect Your Mobile Device
- Connect to Your IMAP Client Application
- Log on to the Amazon WorkMail Web Application

Connect Microsoft Outlook to Your Amazon WorkMail Account

Amazon WorkMail uses auto-discover to configure your Outlook client. To set up your Outlook client, the only information you need is your Amazon WorkMail email address and password. Amazon WorkMail provides integration with the following versions of Microsoft Outlook:

- Microsoft Outlook 2007
- Microsoft Outlook 2010
- Microsoft Outlook 2013
- Microsoft Outlook 2016
- Microsoft Outlook for Mac 2011
- Microsoft Outlook 2016 for Mac

To connect Microsoft Outlook to your Amazon WorkMail account

1. In Microsoft Windows, open **Control Panel**, and choose **User Accounts and Mail (32-bit)**.

2. In the **Mail Setup - Outlook** dialog box, choose **Show Profiles**; in the **Mail** dialog box, choose **Add**.

3. In the **New Profile** dialog box, type **WorkMail** in the **Profile Name** field and choose **OK**.

4. In the **Add New Account** dialog box, enter your Amazon WorkMail email address in the **E-mail Address** field, and choose **Next**. **Note**
   Microsoft Outlook attempts to detect your email server settings. You are prompted to enter your user name and password during this search. Make sure that you enter your full email address as your user name. If Microsoft Outlook prompts you to configure server settings in the **Allow this website to configure...** dialog box, select the **Don't ask me about this website again** check box and choose **Allow**.

5. After Microsoft Outlook detects your email server settings and sets up your account, you'll see a message that says your account is ready for use. Choose Finish.

   For more information about adding accounts in Microsoft Outlook, see Set Up E-Mail in Outlook 2010 or Outlook 2013.

To connect Microsoft Outlook for Mac to your Amazon WorkMail account

1. In Microsoft Outlook 2016 for Mac, do one of the following:

   - If this is the first account you're creating in Outlook for Mac, on the **Welcome** screen, choose **Add Email Account**, enter your email address, and choose **Continue**. Under **Choose the provider**, choose **Exchange**.
   - If you already have an email account for a different email address, in the **Tools** menu, choose **Accounts**. In the **Accounts** dialog box, choose **+** (plus sign) and **New Account**. Enter your **Email Address** and choose **Continue**. Under **Choose the provider**, choose **Exchange**.

2. In the **Enter your Exchange account information** dialog box, for **Method**, choose **User Name and Password** and enter your email address.

3. For **Domain\Username or Email**, enter your email address, and for **Password**, enter your password.

4. Choose **Add Account** to complete setup. **Note**
   Microsoft Outlook attempts to detect your email server settings.
   If Microsoft Outlook prompts you to allow the server to configure your settings, select the **Always use my response for this server** check box and choose **Allow**.

   After your account is successfully set up, it is listed in the **Accounts** dialog box.

   For more information about adding accounts in Microsoft Outlook for Mac 2011, see Add an email account to Outlook for Mac 2011. For more information about adding accounts in Microsoft Outlook 2016 for Mac, see Add an email account to Outlook 2016 for Mac.

Connect Your Mail App on Windows 10

If you have the Mail app on Windows 10, you can add your Amazon WorkMail account.

To connect your Amazon WorkMail account to your Mail app

1. Open Mail and choose **Accounts**.

2. Choose **Add Account**, **Advanced Setup**.

3. Choose **Exchange ActiveSync** and fill in the following values:
   [See the AWS documentation website for more details]

4. Choose **Sign in**.

Connect Your Mail App on macOS

If you have the Mail app on macOS, you can add your Amazon WorkMail account.

To connect your Amazon WorkMail account to your Mail app

1. Open Mail, and then do one of the following:

   - If you don't have a Mail account: Create an account and choose **Exchange** for the account type.
   - If you already have a Mail account: On the **Mail** menu, choose **Preferences**. On the **Accounts** tab, choose the plus sign (+) at the bottom of the navigation pane to open the **Add Account** window.

2. Fill in your full name, email address, and password. Choose **Continue**.

3. The Mail app uses the information above to set up your email account automatically.

Connect Your iOS Device

Amazon WorkMail supports Microsoft Exchange ActiveSync for integration with iOS devices. To connect your iOS device to your Amazon WorkMail email account, you only need your Amazon WorkMail email address and password.

Note
If your organization has enabled mobile device management, you may be required to set a password to connect your device.

To connect your Amazon WorkMail account to your iOS device

1. On your iOS device, choose **Settings**, and then scroll down to **Accounts & Passwords** (or in older versions, **Mail**).

2. Choose **Add Account** and **Exchange**. **Note**
   In older versions, select **Accounts**, **Add Account**, **Exchange**.

3. In iOS 11, enter your Amazon WorkMail email address and a description for the account, and choose **Next**. In the dialog box, choose **Sign in** and enter the password of your email address. **Note**
   In older versions, enter your Amazon WorkMail email address, password, and a description for the account, and choose **Next**.
   In iOS 11, automatic configuration works if you use a complimentary domain (such as awsapps.com) or if you use a customer domain and Autodiscover Phase 2. For more information, see Use AutoDiscover to Configure Endpoints.
   If your account cannot be found, you are prompted to provide the name of your Exchange server, domain, user name, and password. For more information, see Manually Connect Your Mobile Device. In the Exchange confirmation dialog box, select the items to synchronize with your device, and then choose **Save**.

   You can now use your iOS device with your Amazon WorkMail account. **Note**
   Amazon WorkMail does not support draft synchronization with iOS devices.

Connect Your Android Device

Amazon WorkMail supports Exchange ActiveSync for integration with Android devices, so to connect your Android device to your Amazon WorkMail email account you need your Amazon WorkMail email address and password.

To connect your Amazon WorkMail account to your Android device

1. On your Android device, choose **Apps**, **Email**, **Add Account**, and then **Exchange**.

2. In the **Exchange** dialog box, enter your Amazon WorkMail email address, password, and a description for the account, and then choose **Next. Note**
   If your account cannot be found, you are prompted to provide the name of your Exchange server, domain, user name, and password. For more information, see Manually Connect Your Mobile Device.

3. In the Exchange confirmation dialog box, select the items to synchronize with your device, and then choose **Save**.

   You can now use your Android email app with your Amazon WorkMail email account. **Note**
   Amazon WorkMail does not support draft synchronization with Android devices.

Manually Connect Your Mobile Device

If your mobile device doesn't support auto-discover or if automatic configuration failed, you can manually configure the client by providing the following information:

Required Information	Description
Type of account	Exchange
Protocol	ActiveSync
Domain	Your domain
Username	Email address associated with your Amazon WorkMail account
Password	Your password
Server	The endpoint matching the region where your mailbox is located: [See the AWS documentation website for more details] If you don't know the region where your mailbox is located, contact your system administrator.

Connect to Your IMAP Client Application

You can connect any IMAP-compatible client software to Amazon WorkMail by providing the following information:

Required Information	Description
Type of account	IMAP
Protocol	IMAPS
Port	993
Secure connection	Required; SSL
Incoming username	Email address associated with your Amazon WorkMail account
Incoming password	Your password
Incoming server	The endpoint matching the region where your mailbox is located: [See the AWS documentation website for more details] If you don't know the region where your mailbox is located, contact your system administrator.

To send emails, you also need to configure an outgoing SMTP server in your client software.

Required Information	Description
Protocol	SMTPS (SMTP, encrypted with TLS)
Port	465
Secure connection	Required; SSL (STARTTLS not supported)
Outgoing username	Email address associated with your Amazon WorkMail account
Outgoing password	Your password
Outgoing server	The endpoint matching the region where your mailbox is located: [See the AWS documentation website for more details] If you don't know the region where your mailbox is located, contact your system administrator.

Log on to the Amazon WorkMail Web Application

Amazon WorkMail has a web-based application that you can use to access your Amazon WorkMail account from a web browser. The Amazon WorkMail web application includes integrated applications such as mail, calendar, and contacts. To get started with the Amazon WorkMail web application, you need a broadband internet connection and the latest version of one of the following web browsers:

- Google Chrome
- Mozilla Firefox
- Apple Safari
- Microsoft Edge
- Microsoft Internet Explorer

Your Amazon WorkMail system administrator provides you with your initial login credentials, which consist of a username and a password. To recover a lost or forgotten password, contact your administrator.

You also need your unique Amazon WorkMail web application URL, which contains an alias—the unique name chosen for your mail domain when your organization was added.

To locate your Amazon WorkMail web application URL

1. Open the Amazon WorkMail console at https://console.aws.amazon.com/workmail/.

2. In the navigation panel, choose **Organization settings**.

The **Web application** URL is in the **General settings** tab and looks like this: https://*alias*.awsapps.com/mail.

To log on to the Amazon WorkMail web application

1. In the address bar of your browser, type or paste the web application URL.

2. On the Amazon WorkMail web application login screen, enter your username and password, and then choose **Sign In**.

3. After you log in to the Amazon WorkMail web application, you are ready to work.

The Amazon WorkMail web application is made up of the following sections:

1. **Shortcut Bar**—Contains shortcuts to the Mail, Calendar, and Contacts applications in the Amazon WorkMail web application. The currently active application is highlighted in the shortcut bar.

2. **Navigation Pane**—Allows you to navigate within the active application, such as the folders in the email application or the calendars within the calendar application.

3. **Menu Bar**—Controls the most important functions for the Mail, Calendar, and Contacts applications. The controls that are available vary depending on the application that is active. Depending on the application in use, you can create new items, change the view, print, or access the address book.

4. **Contents Pane**—Where data is displayed, such as the contents of an email message, the calendar, or the contacts list. You can use the **Search** field at the top of the results pane to search for items in the current folder. You can use the tabs to switch between email messages, appointments, and contacts. You can choose the plus button (+) in the row of tabs to add a new item in its own tab. The item created depends on the active application. For example, choosing the plus button in the mail application creates a new email; in the calendar application, it creates a new appointment, and so on.

For more information, about how to change the language that appears at any time, see General Tab.

Working with Email

You can send, read, reply to, and delete email in Amazon WorkMail.

To send email

You can create and send email to one or more recipients, include attachments, set the priority, and add flags to indicate importance.

1. In the Amazon WorkMail web application, press **Tab** until the screen reader reads *Create new item, button list item*. Press **Enter**.

2. The message opens with the cursor in the **To** field. Add a contact using one of the following methods:
   - **Add a contact from the Address Book**. Hold down **Shift+Tab** to highlight the **To** field, then press **Enter**. Start typing a contact's name into the field. A list of suggested matching names is provided. Use the **Up/Down** arrows to navigate through the list. Press **Enter** to select a contact. To add multiple contacts, continue selecting names; the separator is added automatically.
   - **Search for the contact**. You can search for a contact using the Using the Global Address Book.
     Note
     If a recipient's name is ambiguous or has multiple matches, the screen reader reads *Check ambiguous names, dialog*. Select the correct recipient from the list provided.

3. Press **Tab** to navigate to and set the **Cc**, **Bcc**, **From**, **Subject**, **High Priority**, **Low Priority**, **Set Flag**, and **Options** fields for the message.

4. Press **Tab** to get to the message composition field and type your message.

5. To send the message, use **Shift+Tab** until the screen reader reads *Send button*. Press **Enter** to send.
   Note
   If there are any unresolved recipients, the screen reader reads *Not all recipients could be resolved. OK button*. Review the recipients and correct them as needed.

To read email

Reading the email in your inbox.

1. In the Amazon WorkMail web application, press **Tab** and, depending on your screen reader, use the **Up/Down** arrow keys or table navigation to navigate through the messages.

2. Select the row of the message to read. Press **Enter** to open the message in a new tab.

3. Press **Tab** to navigate through the **Response** toolbar. Use the **Up/Down** arrows to navigate through the page, and read the body of the message line-by-line.

To reply to email

1. In the Amazon WorkMail web application, press **Tab** to navigate to the message. Use the **Up/Down** arrows to navigate scroll through the messages in the table.

2. Select the row of the message to read. Press **Enter** to open the message in a new tab.

3. Use **Tab** to read the **Response** toolbar. You can select **Reply**, **Reply All**, **Forward**, or **Delete**. You can navigate using the screen reader or the following keyboard shortcuts:
   [See the AWS documentation website for more details]

4. Type your reply in the message form. To send the message, use **Shift+Tab** until the screen reader reads *Send button*. Press **Enter** to send.

To delete email

When you no longer need a message, you can delete it. This also helps free up space in your inbox.

1. In the Amazon WorkMail web application, press **Tab** to navigate to the message. Use the **Up/Down** arrows to scroll through the messages in the table.

2. Select the row of the message to read. Press **Enter** to open the message in a new tab.

3. To delete the message, press **Delete** on your keyboard. You can also navigate to the **Delete** button using **Shift+Tab**.

To copy and move email

You can copy email or move it from one folder to another.

1. In the Amazon WorkMail web application, press **Tab** to navigate to the message. Use the **Up/Down** arrows to scroll through the messages in the table.

2. Press **Shift+Tab** until the screen reader reads *Copy/Move button*.

3. In the **Copy/move message** dialog, choose the destination folder. Then use **Tab** to select either **Copy** or **Move**.

4. Press **Enter** to complete the action.

To search for email

You can search all the folders to find a specific message.

1. In the Amazon WorkMail web application, press **Tab** to navigate until the screen reader reads *Mail action toolbar, toolbar, search text, edit text.*

2. Type the keyword into the search bar, and press **Enter**.

3. To clear the search term, press **Tab** until the screen reader reads *Clear search button* and the focus moves to the **X** button, then press **Enter**. To search again, repeat the process.

Send an Email Message

You can create and send a message to one or more recipients, include attachments, set the priority, or add a flag to indicate that the message is important.

To send a message

1. In the Amazon WorkMail web application, choose the mail icon on the shortcut bar.

2. On the menu bar, choose **+ New item** and **New email. Tip**
   You can also choose the plus sign (+) on the tab bar.

3. To add recipients, for **To**, type one or more names. Amazon WorkMail suggests previously used email addresses. You can remove suggestions from this list by selecting a name and choosing **Delete**.

   To add users from the address book or to add them to the **CC** or **BCC** fields, choose **To**, and select one or more users from the address book as appropriate.

4. To add an attachment, choose **Attach. Note**
   The following attachment types aren't supported:
   Unsupported Attachment Types
   [See the AWS documentation website for more details]

5. To mark the message as important or high priority, low priority, or for follow-up, choose the exclamation mark (!), down arrow, or flag icon.

   ! High priority

   ↓ Low priority

   ▶ Follow-up

6. To mark the message for follow-up or as a completed task, choose the flag or the checkmark icon.

   ▶ Follow-up

   ✔ Complete

   ▷ Clear

7. To save the message as a draft in the **Drafts** folder, choose **Save**.

8. Enter your text in the lower half of the contents pane, and choose **Send**.

If your IT administrator has enabled you to use Amazon WorkDocs, you can add files from Amazon WorkDocs to messages and send them to other recipients.

To attach a file from Amazon WorkDocs

1. In the Amazon WorkMail web application, choose the new mail icon + on the shortcut bar.

2. Choose **Attach** and browse to the **Amazon WorkDocs** folder.

3. Select the files to attach and choose **Attach Files**.

Note
The total size of the attached files can't exceed 25 MB.

Send an Encrypted or Signed Email

With S/MIME, you can send signed or encrypted emails inside and outside of your organization. After you configure S/MIME in the email client settings, all emails that you send are automatically signed. Encryption options depend on different email clients and respective platforms.

Note
The Amazon WorkMail web app client is not supported.

To configure S/MIME in Windows Outlook

1. Get the certificate (*.p12) file from your administrator or third-party provider and save it to a folder.

2. Right-click the file and choose **Install PFX**.

3. Choose **Current User, Next**, select the *.p12 file, and then choose **Next**.

4. Enter the password and choose **Next**.

5. Make sure that **Automatically select the certificate store...** is selected and choose **Next**.

6. Choose **Finish**.

7. Perform the following steps in Windows Outlook:

    1. Choose **File, Options, Trust Center, Trust Center Settings...**, **Email Security**, and **Settings**.

    2. In the **Change Email Security** dialog box, choose **Choose...** and select the installed certificate.

    3. Choose **OK**, select one or all applicable options, and choose **OK**.

8. If all email recipients have certificates in the Global Address List (GAL) or Contacts, then all emails sent are automatically encrypted. Otherwise, you receive a warning message and can decide to send an unencrypted message or cancel.

To configure S/MIME in iOS Mail

1. Get the certificate (*.p12) file from your administrator or third-party provider in an email.

2. Open the email attachment and choose **Install**.

3. Enter the PIN and follow the instructions.

4. Choose **Settings, Mail, Accounts**, select your account, and then choose **Account, Advanced Settings**.

5. Enable S/MIME and choose one or both of the options to sign or encrypt emails. If you chose **Encrypt by Default**, then all emails sent are automatically encrypted.

6. When you type an email address in the **To** field, iOS loads the user certificate from the Global Address List (GAL) or from Contacts. If the certificate is not found, then the red unlocked icon means that the email can't be encrypted.

To configure S/MIME in Android Nine and the Samsung Mobile devices native mail app

1. Get the certificate (*.pfx or *.p12) file from your administrator or third-party provider in an email.

2. Download the attached certificates.

3. Open the Android Nine app and choose **Email Settings, Accounts**, select your account, and then choose **Security options**.

4. To enable encryption, choose **Encrypt ongoing emails**. Under **Email encryption cert**, choose **Install**, select your certificate used for encrypting your email message, and then choose **Allow**. **Note**
If you allow **Email encryption cert**, when you send an email, the app loads and validates the user certificate from the Global Address List (GAL) or from a contact. If the certificate is found for the recipient,

the email is sent as encrypted. Otherwise, an error is displayed and the email is not sent. You must disable the **Email encryption cert** setting.

5. To enable signing, choose **Sign all outgoing emails**. Under **Email signing cert**, choose **Install**, select your certificate used for signing your email message, and then choose **Allow**.

To configure S/MIME in Outlook for Mac 2016

1. Install the certificate on macOS:

   1. Get the certificate (*.p12) file from your administrator or third party provider, and save the file to a folder.

   2. Double-click the certificate file to open **Keychain Access** and approve to add the certificate to your keychain.

   3. In the list of certificates in your keychain, view the newly installed certificate.

2. In Outlook for Mac, choose **Tools**, **Accounts**, select your account, and then choose **Advanced**, **Security**.

3. In **Digital signing** and **Encryption**, choose the newly installed certificate from the list and choose from the following options:

   - To sign all outgoing messages by default, choose **Sign outgoing messages**.
   - To encrypt all outgoing messages by default, choose **Encrypt outgoing messages**.
   - To make sure that your signed message can be viewed by all recipients and mail applications, choose **Send digitally signed messages as clear text**.
   - To enable recipients to send encrypted messages to you, choose **Include my certificates in signed messages**.

4. Choose **OK**.

Note
To send an encrypted email to the group, manually expand the group.

Delete an Email Message

When you no longer need an email message, you can delete it. Deleting unwanted email also helps you to free up space in your inbox.

To delete a message

1. In the Amazon WorkMail web application, choose the mail icon on the shortcut bar.

2. Do one of the following:

   - In the contents pane, select a message and press the **Delete** key.
   - In the contents pane, open the message and choose **Delete**.
   - In the **Message** tab, choose **Delete**.

If you mistakenly delete a message, calendar item, or contact, you can restore it. All deleted email, calendar items, and contacts are stored in the Deleted Items folder in the application.

Note

You can only restore items that are still in the Deleted Items folder. If you've emptied the Deleted Items folder, those items are unrecoverable.

To restore a deleted item

1. In the Amazon WorkMail web application, choose the mail icon on the shortcut bar.

2. In the **Deleted Items** folder, select the message to restore and choose **Copy/Move**. **Tip** You can also choose the plus sign (+) on the tab bar.

3. In the **Copy/move messages** dialog box, select the destination folder and choose **Move**.

Copy or Move an Email Message

You can copy or move a message from one folder to another.

To copy or move a message

1. In the Amazon WorkMail web application, choose the mail icon on the shortcut bar.

2. Do one of the following:

   - To copy an item, select the message in the contents pane and choose **Copy/Move**.
   - To copy more than one message, press the **Ctrl** key while you select each message in the contents pane, and then choose **Copy/Move**.
   - To move a single message, drag the item to its new location. **Tip**
     The folder names directly under the dragged message are highlighted and show the target location when you release the message.
   - To move multiple consecutive messages, press the **Shift** key while you select all the messages to move, and then drag them to the desired folder.
   - To move messages that are not consecutive, press the **Ctrl** key while you select each message to move, release the **Ctrl** key, and then drag them into the designated folder.

3. In the **Copy/move messages** dialog box, select the destination folder and choose either **Copy** or **Move**.

Download Attachments

You can download attachments that you've received and save them to your hard drive.

To download attachments

1. In the Amazon WorkMail web application, choose the mail icon on the shortcut bar.

2. Open the context (right-click) menu for the attachment and choose **Download**.

If your IT administrator has enabled you to use Amazon WorkDocs, you can also save your email attachments to Amazon WorkDocs for archiving or collaboration purposes.

To save an attachment to Amazon WorkDocs

1. Open the message with the attachment to save.

2. Open the attachment and choose **Save to WorkDocs**. The file is saved to your **My Documents** folder in Amazon WorkDocs.

Print an Email Message

If you have a printer attached to your computer and your computer is set up to print documents, you can print your messages.

To print a message

1. In the Amazon WorkMail web application, on the shortcut bar, choose the mail icon.

2. In the navigation pane, select the folder that contains the message to print.

3. In the contents pane, select the message to print and choose **Print** on the menu bar.

Send as an Alias

You can send and receive email using an alias configured for you. Recipients outside of your organization then see the sender as your alias address instead of your primary address. For information about configuring aliases, see Edit User Email Addresses.

Note

If you send an email from an alias to someone in your organization, the message is still received from your primary address.

To send an email from an alias

1. In the Amazon WorkMail web application, choose the mail icon on the shortcut bar and choose **+ New item**, **New email**.

2. For **From**, type the alias from which to send email. **Tip**
   To include a display name, use the SMTP standard format "Your Name <youralias@domain.com>".

3. When you're ready to send the email, choose **Send**.

Open a Shared Inbox

You can open an inbox that another user has shared with you.

To open a shared inbox

1. In the Amazon WorkMail web application, on the shortcut bar, choose the mail icon.

2. At the bottom of the navigation pane, choose **Open other inbox**.

3. In the **Open other folders** dialog box, choose **Name**.

4. For **Address Book**, select the owner of the inbox to open, and choose **OK**.

5. In the **Open other folders** dialog box, for **Folder type**, choose **Inbox**.

6. Choose **Show subfolders**, **OK**.

   The shared mail folders are now visible in the navigation pane. **Note**
   The shared folders are stored in your Amazon WorkMail web application profile. The next time you log in to the Amazon WorkMail web application, the opened folders are still displayed.
   If you receive a message saying "You have insufficient privileges to open this folder.", contact the owner of the folder and ask them to grant you access.
   To change folder permissions, in the navigation pane, right-click the folder, choose **Properties, Permissions**.

7. To close a shared folder, open the context (right-click) menu for the shared folder, and choose **Close store**.

Open a Full Access Mailbox

You can open all the folders in a mailbox for which your administrator has given you full access.

To open a full access mailbox

1. In the Amazon WorkMail web application, on the shortcut bar, choose the mail icon.

2. At the bottom of the navigation pane, choose **Open other inbox**.

3. In the **Open other folders** dialog box, choose **Name**.

4. For **Address Book**, select the owner of the mailbox to open, and choose **OK**.

5. In the **Open other folders** dialog box, for **Folder type**, choose **All**.

The shared mailbox is now visible in the navigation pane.

Note
The shared mailboxes are stored in your Amazon WorkMail web application profile. The next time you log in to the Amazon WorkMail web application, the opened mailboxes are still displayed.
If you receive a message saying "`You have insufficient privileges to open this folder.`", contact your administrator and ask them to grant you access.

To close a shared mailbox, open the context (right-click) menu for the shared mailbox, and then choose **Close store**.

Working with Folders

You can create folders to organize your email, contacts, and calendar items.

To create a new folder

1. In the Amazon WorkMail web application, press **Shift+Tab** until the screen reader reads *New item pop-up button*. Press **Enter** to select it. Use the **Up/Down** arrows to select **New folder**. The cursor focus is in the **Name** field.

2. Enter the name of your new folder. Navigate through the items using **Tab**.

3. Select the destination folder of the new folder. Navigate through the items using the **Up/Down** arrows.

4. Press **Enter** to select a destination folder, press **Tab** to navigate to **Ok**, and then press **Enter** to save.

To delete a folder

You can delete folders you're no longer using. Deleting folders also deletes the email in the folders.

1. In the Amazon WorkMail web application, press **Shift+Tab** until the screen reader reads *Inbox*. Press **Enter** to select it. Use the **Up/Down** arrow keys to select the folder to delete.

2. On the confirmation screen, the screen reader reads *Are you sure you want to move the folder [subfolder] and all of its contents into the **Deleted items** folder?*.

3. The cursor focus is on the **Yes** option. Press **Enter** to delete the folder.

To copy or move folders

You can copy and move folders within Amazon WorkMail.

1. In the Amazon WorkMail web application, press **Shift+Tab** until the screen reader reads *Inbox*. Use the **Up/Down** arrow keys to select the folder to be copied or moved.

2. Press **Shift+F10** to open the context menu, and select **Copy**.

3. In the dialog box press **Shift+Tab** to move to the destination folder, then use the **Up/Down** arrows to choose the destination folder.

4. Press **Tab** and **Enter** to copy or move the folder.

Create a New Folder

You can create folders to organize your email, contacts, and calendar items.

To create a new folder

1. In the Amazon WorkMail web application, on the shortcut bar, choose the mail icon.

2. On the task bar, choose **+ New item**, **New folder**.

3. In the **Create New Folder** dialog box, for **Name**, enter the name of the new folder.

4. For **Folder contains**, select the type of contents for the folder to contain.

5. For **Select where to place the folder**, select the target location and choose **OK**.

Delete a Folder

You can delete a folder that you no longer need. Deleting a folder also deletes any items in the folder.

To delete a folder

1. In the Amazon WorkMail web application, on the shortcut bar, choose the mail icon.

2. In the navigation pane, open the context (right-click) menu for the folder, and choose **Delete**.

Empty the Deleted Items Folder

If your inbox is full and you're out of space, you can empty the Deleted Items folder to free-up space. When you empty the Deleted Items folder, you cannot recover or undelete those items.

To empty the Deleted Items folder

1. In the Amazon WorkMail web application, on the shortcut bar, choose the mail icon.

2. In the navigation pane, open the context (right-click) menu for the **Deleted Items** folder, and choose **Empty folder**.

Mark Items as Read or Unread

You can mark all items in a folder as read or unread.

To mark all items in a folder as read

1. In the Amazon WorkMail web application, on the shortcut bar, choose the mail icon.

2. In the navigation pane, open the context (right-click) menu for the folder, and choose **Mark all read**.

To mark all items in a folder as unread

1. In the Amazon WorkMail web application, on the shortcut bar, choose the mail icon.

2. In the navigation pane, select the folder.

3. In the contents pane, select all items in the folder, open the context (right-click), and then choose **Mark Unread**.

View the Size of a Folder

You can view a folder's size to see how much storage space it takes up.

To view the size of a folder

1. In the Amazon WorkMail web application, on the shortcut bar, choose the mail icon.

2. In the navigation pane, open the context (right-click) menu for a mail folder, and choose **Properties**. **Tip** To see more details about the storage size, including the storage sizes of any subfolders, choose **Details**.

Share an Email Folder with Another User

You can give another user permission to view an email folder.

To share an email folder with another user

1. In the Amazon WorkMail web application, on the shortcut bar, choose the mail icon.

2. In the navigation pane, open the context (right-click) menu for the folder to share, and choose **Properties**.

3. On the **User details** page, under **Permissions**, choose **Add or remove**.

4. Under **Users and groups**, select the user to share your folder and choose » to add them to the **Permissions** list. Choose **Save**.

5. On the **Permissions** tab, select the level of permissions to grant, and choose **Save**.

Open a Shared Email Folder

You can open an email folder that has been shared with you.

To open a shared email folder

1. In the Amazon WorkMail web application, on the shortcut bar, choose the mail icon.

2. In the navigation pane, choose **Open other inbox**.

3. In the **Open other folders** dialog box, choose **Name**.

4. For **Address Book**, select the owner of the inbox to open and choose **OK**.

5. In the **Open other folders** dialog box, for **Folder type**, select the inbox, and choose **OK**.

   The shared mail folders are now visible in the navigation pane. **Note**
   The shared folders are stored in your Amazon WorkMail web application profile. The next time you log in to the Amazon WorkMail web application, the opened folders are still displayed.
   If you receive a message saying "You have insufficient privileges to open this folder.", contact the owner of the folder and ask them to grant you access.
   To change folder permissions, in the navigation pane, open the context (right-click) the folder, choose **Properties**, **Permissions**.

6. To close a shared folder, open the context (right-click) menu for the shared folder, and choose **Close store**.

Copy, Move, or Rename a Folder

You can copy, move, and rename folders.

To copy or move a folder

1. In the Amazon WorkMail web application, on the shortcut bar, choose the mail icon.

2. In the navigation pane, right-click the folder, choose **Copy/move**, select the target folder, and then choose **Copy** or **Move**.

To rename a folder

1. In the Amazon WorkMail web application, on the shortcut bar, choose the mail icon.

2. In the navigation pane, open the context (right-click) menu for the folder, and choose **Rename**.

3. Enter a new name for the folder.

View Folder Permissions

By default, you have full permissions on all of the folders and items that you own. You can share your folders with other users and groups in your organization by changing the permissions for a folder. The folder permissions provide others with different access privileges to the folder and its contents.

To view folder permissions

1. In the Amazon WorkMail web application, on the shortcut bar, choose the mail icon.

2. In the navigation pane, open the context (right-click) menu for the folder, and choose **Properties**.

3. In the **Properties **dialog box, choose the **Permissions** tab.

4. For **Profile**, select a predefined set of permissions, or customize the permissions as needed.

Change a Folder's Permissions

You can set the permissions on a shared folder to specify the actions another user can perform on items in folder you shared with them.

To change a folder's permissions

1. In the Amazon WorkMail web application, on the shortcut bar, choose the mail icon.

2. In the navigation pane, open the context (right-click) menu for the folder, and choose **Properties**.

3. In the **Properties** dialog box, choose **Permissions, Add**.

4. For **Address Book**, select the users or groups in your organization with which to share the folder, and choose **OK**.

5. Select the user or group to which to apply the permissions.

6. For **Profile**, select a predefined set of permissions, or customize the permissions as needed.

7. Repeat steps 5 and 6 for each of the users or groups in the list.

8. Choose **OK**.

Stop Sharing a Folder

If you've shared a folder with another user, you can stop sharing it at any time.

To stop sharing a folder

1. In the Amazon WorkMail web application, on the shortcut bar, choose the mail icon.

2. In the navigation pane, open the context (right-click) menu for the folder, and choose **Properties**.

3. On the **User details** page, under **Permissions**, choose **Add or remove**.

4. For **Permissions**, select the user or group to remove, and choose < <.

5. Repeat as necessary, then choose **Save**.

Working with Calendars

You can create both appointments and meetings in the Amazon WorkMail web application.

An appointment is an item in your calendar that is only applicable to you. No other participants are invited.

A meeting is an item in your calendar that has more than one participant. As soon as you invite a coworker or schedule a resource with any appointment, it automatically becomes a meeting. When you create or edit a meeting in the Amazon WorkMail web application, there are extra controls and buttons for meeting invitations.

Topics

- Change the Calendar View
- Create an Appointment
- Create a Meeting Request
- Edit a Meeting or Appointment
- Move a Meeting or Appointment
- Delete a Meeting or Appointment
- Cancel or Decline a Scheduled Meeting
- Work with Multiple Calendars
- Print Calendar Items
- Share Your Calendar with Another User
- Open a Shared Calendar
- Change Calendar Settings

Change the Calendar View

You can switch the calendar layout to view appointments by day, work week, week, or month.

To change the calendar view

1. In the Amazon WorkMail web application, on the shortcut bar, choose the calendar icon.

2. In the navigation pane, choose **Day**, **Workweek**, **Week**, or **Month**.

Create an Appointment

You can create an appointment and set a reminder that automatically reminds you before the appointment's start date and time.

To create an appointment

1. In the Amazon WorkMail web application, on the shortcut bar, choose the calendar icon.

2. On the menu bar, choose **New appointment**.

3. Enter the following:

   - For **Subject**, enter a subject for the appointment.
   - For **Start** and **End**, specify the start and end times for the appointment.
   - (Optional) For **Location**, specify a location.
   - (Optional) For **Reminder**, set a reminder.

4. Choose **Save and close. Tip**
   You can also create an appointment by double-clicking in the calendar.

Create a Meeting Request

You can create a meeting request that includes attendees and resources, and set a reminder to remind you before the meeting starts.

To create a meeting request

1. In the Amazon WorkMail web application, on the shortcut bar, choose the calendar icon.

2. On the menu bar, choose **New meeting request**.

3. To add one or more attendees, type their names in the **To** field. Amazon WorkMail suggests names from the address book. You can remove suggestions from this list by selecting a name and then pressing **Delete**. To add users from the address book or to add them to the **Required, Optional**, or **Resource** fields, choose **To**, and select one or more users from the address book and add them to the appropriate fields.

4. Enter the following:

   - For **Subject**, enter a subject for the meeting.
   - For **Start** and **End**, specify the start and end times for the meeting.
   - For **Location**, specify a location.
   - (Optional) For **Reminder**, set a reminder.

5. In the lower portion of the meeting invitation, you can add information about the meeting, such as an agenda. To add an attachment to the meeting invitation, choose **Attach**.

6. Choose **Send invitation**.

Edit a Meeting or Appointment

You can edit a meeting or an appointment to make changes.

To edit a meeting or appointment

1. In the Amazon WorkMail web application, on the shortcut bar, select the calendar icon.

2. On the calendar, open the meeting or appointment and edit the meeting as appropriate.

3. If you are the organizer of a meeting, do one of the following:

    - To save your changes and send an update to the other participants, choose **Send invitation**.
    - To save your changes to the meeting without sending an update to the other participants, choose **Save**.

Move a Meeting or Appointment

You can move a meeting or appointment by clicking it and dragging it to a different day or time. You can also edit the meeting or appointment to move it.

To move a meeting or appointment

1. In the Amazon WorkMail web application, on the shortcut bar, select the calendar icon.

2. On the calendar, do one of the following:

   - Drag the meeting or appointment to a different day and time.
   - Open the meeting or appointment and change the date and time.

3. For a meeting, if prompted to send an update to attendees, choose **Yes**.

Delete a Meeting or Appointment

You can delete a meeting or appointment that you no longer plan to hold or attend.

To delete a meeting or appointment

1. In the Amazon WorkMail web application, on the shortcut bar, select the calendar icon.

2. On the calendar, open the context (right-click) menu for the meeting or appointment, and choose **Delete**.

Cancel or Decline a Scheduled Meeting

You can cancel or decline a scheduled meeting.

To cancel or decline a scheduled meeting

1. In the Amazon WorkMail web application, on the shortcut bar, choose the calendar icon.

2. In the calendar, double-click the meeting, and then do one of the following:

   - If you are the meeting organizer, choose **Cancel invitation**.
   - If you are not the organizer, choose **Decline**.

3. In the **Send meeting request cancellation** dialog box, do one of the following:

   - To send a message along with your response, choose **Edit the cancellation before sending**, **OK**.
   - To send your response without comments, choose **Send the cancellation now**, **OK**.

Work with Multiple Calendars

You can open multiple calendars in a single overview. You can open the calendars side by side or in an overlay to see the calendars transparently stacked on top of each other. By default, the calendars are opened side by side.

To work with multiple calendars

1. In the Amazon WorkMail web application, on the shortcut bar, choose the calendar icon.

2. At the bottom of navigation pane, choose **Open other calendars**.

3. In the **Open other folders** dialog box, choose **Name**.

4. In the address book, select the owner of calendar to open and choose **OK**.

5. For **Folder type**, choose **Calendar**.

6. To show the subfolders of the shared calendar, choose **Show subfolders**.

7. Choose **OK**.

8. Repeat steps 1–5 for each calendar to open.

9. To place calendars in the stacked overlay, use the arrow buttons on top of the calendars.

Print Calendar Items

You can print a single appointment or meeting or overviews of a certain time period, such as five or seven days.

To print calendar items

1. In the Amazon WorkMail web application, on the shortcut bar, choose the calendar icon.

2. In the calendar, open the appointment, and then choose **Print**.

To print a calendar overview

1. In the Amazon WorkMail web application, on the shortcut bar, choose the calendar icon.

2. In the calendar, open the appointment.

3. Choose **Print, Print overview. Note**
   You can print overviews from your workweek (5 days) and the entire week (7 days).

Share Your Calendar with Another User

You can give another user permission to view your calendar.

To share your calendar with another user

1. In the Amazon WorkMail web application, on the shortcut bar, choose the calendar icon.

2. In the navigation pane, open the context (right-click) menu for the **Calendar** folder, and choose **Properties**.

3. On the **User details** page, under **Permissions**, choose **Add or remove**.

4. Select the user to share your calendar with and choose » to add them to the **Permissions** list. Choose **Save**.

5. On the **Permissions** tab, select the level of permissions to grant, and choose **Save**.

Open a Shared Calendar

You can set permissions on your calendar and share it with other users.

To open a shared calendar

1. In the Amazon WorkMail web application, on the shortcut bar, choose the calendar icon.

2. At the bottom of the navigation pane, choose **Open other calendars**.

3. In the **Open other folders** dialog box, choose **Name**.

4. In the address book, select the owner of the calendar to open and choose **OK**.

5. For **Folder type**, choose **Calendar**.

6. To show the subfolders of the shared calendar, choose **Show subfolders**.

7. Choose **OK**.

   The shared calendar is now visible in the folder navigation pane. **Note**
   Your opened folders are stored in your Amazon WorkMail web application profile. The next time you log in to the Amazon WorkMail web application, the opened folders are still displayed.
   If you receive a message saying "You have insufficient privileges to open this folder.", contact the owner of the folder and ask them to grant you access.
   To change folder permissions, in the navigation pane, open the context (right-click) menu for the folder and choose **Properties**, **Permissions**.

Change Calendar Settings

You can change the default settings for the calendar.

To change calendar settings

1. On the menu bar, choose **Settings** (the gear icon).

2. In the navigation pane, choose **Calendar**.

3. In the contents pane, update the settings as appropriate.

Working with Contacts

You can add, edit, delete, copy, and print contacts, as well as share contacts with other users.

Topics

- Create a Contact
- Edit a Contact
- Delete a Contact
- Copy or Move a Contact
- Create a Distribution List
- Print a Contact
- Share Your Contacts with Another User
- Open Shared Contacts

Create a Contact

You can create a contact and mark them as private so that they cannot be seen by anyone that you share your contacts with.

Microsoft Outlook users can import contacts from a .csv file.

To create a contact

1. In the Amazon WorkMail web application, on the shortcut bar, choose the contacts icon.

2. Do one of the following:
   - In the row of tabs in the contents pane, choose the + (plus sign).
   - On the menu bar, choose **+ New item**, **New contact**.

3. In the contents pane, enter the contact's information in the appropriate fields.

4. To make the contact private and hide the contact from anyone who has access to your **Contacts** folder, select the **Private** check box.

5. When you're finished editing, choose **Save**.

Edit a Contact

You can edit your contacts to update their information.

To edit a contact

1. In the Amazon WorkMail web application, on the shortcut bar, choose the contacts icon.

2. In the navigation pane, under **My Contacts**, choose **Contacts**.

3. In the contents pane, open the contact to edit.

4. Update the contact information as appropriate, and choose **Save**.

Delete a Contact

When you no longer need contacts, you can delete them.

To delete a contact

1. In the Amazon WorkMail web application, on the shortcut bar, choose the contacts icon.

2. In the navigation pane, under **My Contacts**, choose **Contacts**.

3. In the contents pane, open the context (right-click) menu for the contact and choose **Delete**. **Note**
   To restore a contact that you deleted by mistake, drag the contact from the **Deleted Items** folder back to the **Contacts** folder.

Copy or Move a Contact

You can copy or move a contact to another folder.

To copy or move a contact

1. In the Amazon WorkMail web application, on the shortcut bar, choose the contacts icon.

2. In the navigation pane, under **My Contacts**, choose **Contacts**.

3. Select the contact, choose **Copy/Move**, select the destination folder, and then choose either **Copy** or **Move**.

Create a Distribution List

You can create a distribution list (such as sales) that includes all of the people in a group.

To create a distribution list

1. In the Amazon WorkMail web application, on the shortcut bar, choose the contacts icon.

2. In the navigation pane, under **My Contacts**, select the **Contacts** folder in which to add the new distribution list.

3. On the menu bar, choose **+ New item**, **New distribution list**.

4. In the contents pane, for **Distribution list name**, enter a name for the distribution list.

5. To hide the distribution list from anyone with whom you have shared your contacts folder, select the **Private** check box.

6. Under **Members**, choose **Add from address book** to add new members from the address book to the distribution list. Or you can choose **Add new member** to add a new contact to the distribution list.

7. Choose **Save and close**.

Print a Contact

If you have a printer configured to print documents from your computer, you can print your contacts.

To print a contact

1. In the Amazon WorkMail web application, on the shortcut bar, select the contacts icon.

2. In the navigation pane, under **My Contacts**, select the **Contacts** folder that contains the contact to print.

3. In the contents pane, double-click the contact to print. On the menu bar, choose **Print**.

Share Your Contacts with Another User

You can give another user permission to view your contacts.

To share your contacts with another user

1. In the Amazon WorkMail web application, on the shortcut bar, select the contacts icon.

2. In the navigation pane, open the context (right-click) menu for the **Contacts** folder, and choose **Properties**.

3. On the **User details** page, under **Permissions**, choose **Add or remove**.

4. Select the user to share your contacts with and choose » to add them to the **Permissions** list. Choose **Save**.

5. On the **Permissions** tab, select the level of permissions to grant, and choose **Save**.

Open Shared Contacts

You can open contacts that other users have shared with you.

To open shared contacts

1. In the Amazon WorkMail web application, on the shortcut bar, choose the contacts icon.

2. At the bottom of the navigation pane, choose **Open other contacts**.

3. In the **Open other folders** dialog box, choose **Name** to open the address book.

4. Select the owner of contacts to open, and choose **OK**.

5. For **Folder type**, choose **Contacts**.

6. To view the subfolders of the shared contacts, choose **Show subfolders**.

7. Choose **OK**.

   The shared contacts are now visible in the folder navigation pane. **Note**
   Your opened folders are stored in your Amazon WorkMail web application profile. The next time you log in to the Amazon WorkMail web application, the opened folders are still displayed.
   If you receive a message saying that "You have insufficient privileges to open this folder.", contact the owner of the folder and ask them to grant you access.
   To change folder permissions, in the navigation pane, open the context (right-click) menu for the folder, and choose **Properties**, **Permissions**.

Working with Delegates

You can specify another user as a delegate who can send email on your behalf. For example, if your coworker grants the appropriate permissions to you, you can send emails and schedule meetings on their behalf. In this case, an email or meeting request is sent with the following in the **From** field: "**you** on behalf of **coworker**".

You can specify delegates in Microsoft Outlook. To do this, connect to your Outlook account, and then choose **File**, **Account Settings**, and **Delegate Access**.

Topics

- Send Email on Behalf of Someone Else
- Send Email as Someone Else
- Schedule a Meeting on Behalf of Someone Else
- Share Your Inbox with Another User

Send Email on Behalf of Someone Else

You can send email on another user's behalf if they've made you their delegate.

To send email on behalf of someone else

1. In the Amazon WorkMail web application, on the shortcut bar, choose the mail icon.

2. On the menu bar, choose **+ New item**, **New email**. **Tip**
   You can also choose the plus sign (+) on the tab bar.

3. Under the **To** field, choose **From**.

4. For **From**, enter the name of the person for whom you are sending email.

5. In the contents pane, type your message and choose **Send**.

The mailbox owner appears in the **From:** header, and you appear in the **Sender:** header.

Note
If you have not been granted delegation permissions for the person you specified in the **From** field, you receive an email message in your own inbox indicating that you don't have the required permissions.

Send Email as Someone Else

You can send email as another user or group if your administrator has granted you the **Send As** permission.

To send email as someone else

1. In the Amazon WorkMail web application, on the shortcut bar, choose the mail icon.

2. On the menu bar, choose **+ New item**, **New email**. **Tip**
   You can also choose the plus sign (+) on the tab bar.

3. Under the **To** field, choose **From**.

4. For **From**, enter the name of the person or group for whom you are sending the email.

5. In the contents pane, type your message and choose **Send**.

The mailbox owner appears in both the **From:** and **Sender:** headers.

Note
If you have not been granted **Send As** permissions for the person or group you specified in the **From** field, you receive an email message in your own inbox indicating that you don't have the required permissions.

Schedule a Meeting on Behalf of Someone Else

If another user has made you their delegate, you can schedule meetings on their behalf.

To schedule a meeting on behalf of someone else

1. In the Amazon WorkMail web application, on the shortcut bar, choose the calendar icon.

2. At the bottom of the navigation pane, choose **Open other calendars**, **Name**.

3. In the address book, select the owner of the calendar to open and choose **OK**.

4. For **Folder type**, choose **Calendar**. To show the subfolders of the shared calendar, choose **Show subfolders**.Choose **OK**.

   The shared calendar is now visible in the folder navigation pane. **Note**
   Your opened folders are stored in your Amazon WorkMail web application profile. The next time that you log in to the Amazon WorkMail web application, the opened folders are still displayed.
   If you receive a message saying that "You have insufficient privileges to open this folder." contact the owner of the folder and ask them to grant you access.
   To change folder permissions, in the navigation pane, open the context (right-click) menu for the folder and choose **Properties**, **Permissions**.

5. To create a meeting request, open the day and time on the calendar when the meeting should occur.

6. To add one or more attendees, type their names into the **To** field. Amazon WorkMail suggests names from the address book. You can remove suggestions from this list by selecting a name and then pressing **Delete**. To add users from the address book or to add them to the **Required**, **Optional**, or **Resource** fields, choose **To**, and select one or more users from the address book and add them to the **Required**, **Optional**, or **Resource** fields as appropriate.

7. Enter values for the following:

   - For **Subject**, enter a subject for the meeting.
   - For **Start** and **End**, specify the start and end times for the meeting.
   - For **Location**, specify a location.
   - (Optional) For **Reminder**, set a reminder.

8. In the lower portion of the meeting invitation, you can add information about the meeting, such as an agenda. To add an attachment to the meeting invitation, choose **Attach**.

9. When you're ready to send the meeting invitation, choose **Send invitation**.

Share Your Inbox with Another User

You can give another user permissions to view your inbox.

To share your inbox with another user

1. In the Amazon WorkMail web application, on the shortcut bar, choose the mail icon.

2. In the navigation pane, open the context (right-click) menu for **Inbox**, and choose **Properties**.

3. On the **User details** page, under **Permissions**, choose **Add or remove**.

4. Under **Users and groups**, select the user to share your inbox and choose » to add them to the **Permissions** list. Choose **Save**.

5. On the **Permissions** tab, select the level of permissions to grant, and choose **Save**.

Working with Notifications

With the Amazon WorkMail Push Notifications API, you can receive push notifications about changes in your mailbox, including new email and calendar updates. You can register the URLs (or push notification responders) to receive notifications. With this feature, developers can create responsive applications for Amazon WorkMail users, as applications are quickly notified about changes from a user's mailbox.

For more information, see Notification subscriptions, mailbox events, and EWS in Exchange.

You can subscribe specific folders, such as Inbox or Calendar, or all folders for mailbox change events (including NewMail, Created, and Modified).

Client libraries such as the EWS Java API or the Managed EWS C# API can be used to access this feature. A complete sample application of a push responder, developed using AWS Lambda and API Gateway (using the AWS Serverless framework), is available here. It uses the EWS Java API.

The following is a sample push subscription request:

```
1  <?xml version="1.0" encoding="UTF-8"?>
2  <soap:Envelope xmlns:soap="http://schemas.xmlsoap.org/soap/envelope/" xmlns:t="http://schemas.
      microsoft.com/exchange/services/2006/types">
3    <soap:Body>
4      <m:Subscribe xmlns:m="http://schemas.microsoft.com/exchange/services/2006/messages">
5        <m:PushSubscriptionRequest>
6          <t:FolderIds>
7            <t:DistinguishedFolderId Id="inbox" />
8          </t:FolderIds>
9          <t:EventTypes>
10           <t:EventType>NewMailEvent</t:EventType>
11           <t:EventType>CopiedEvent</t:EventType>
12           <t:EventType>CreatedEvent</t:EventType>
13           <t:EventType>DeletedEvent</t:EventType>
14           <t:EventType>ModifiedEvent</t:EventType>
15           <t:EventType>MovedEvent</t:EventType>
16         </t:EventTypes>
17         <t:StatusFrequency>1</t:StatusFrequency>
18         <t:URL>https://YOUR_PUSH_RESPONDER_URL</t:URL>
19       </m:PushSubscriptionRequest>
20     </m:Subscribe>
21   </soap:Body>
22 </soap:Envelope>
```

The following is a successful subscription request result:

```
1  <?xml version="1.0" encoding="UTF-8"?>
2  <soap:Envelope xmlns:soap="http://schemas.xmlsoap.org/soap/envelope/" xmlns:xsd="http://www.w3.
      org/2001/XMLSchema" xmlns:xsi="http://www.w3.org/2001/XMLSchema-instance">
3    <Header xmlns="http://schemas.xmlsoap.org/soap/envelope/">
4      <ServerVersionInfo xmlns="http://schemas.microsoft.com/exchange/services/2006/types"
          MajorVersion="14" MinorVersion="2" MajorBuildNumber="390" Version="Exchange2010_SP2"
          MinorBuildNumber="3" />
5    </Header>
6    <soap:Body>
7      <m:SubscribeResponse xmlns:m="http://schemas.microsoft.com/exchange/services/2006/messages
          " xmlns:t="http://schemas.microsoft.com/exchange/services/2006/types">
8        <m:ResponseMessages>
9          <m:SubscribeResponseMessage ResponseClass="Success">
```

```
10          <m:ResponseCode>NoError</m:ResponseCode>
11          <m:SubscriptionId>hKJETtoAdi9PPWOtZDQ4MThmMDoVYB</m:SubscriptionId>
12          <m:Watermark>AAAAAAA=</m:Watermark>
13        </m:SubscribeResponseMessage>
14      </m:ResponseMessages>
15    </m:SubscribeResponse>
16  </soap:Body>
17 </soap:Envelope>
```

Afterwards, notifications are sent to the URL specified in the subscription request. The following is a sample notification:

```
1  <soap:Envelope
2      xmlns:soap="http://schemas.xmlsoap.org/soap/envelope/">
3    <soap:Header>
4      <t:RequestServerVersion
5          xmlns:t="http://schemas.microsoft.com/exchange/services/2006/types"
6          xmlns:m="http://schemas.microsoft.com/exchange/services/2006/messages" Version="
                Exchange2010_SP2">
7      </t:RequestServerVersion>
8    </soap:Header>
9    <soap:Body>
10     <m:SendNotification
11         xmlns:t="http://schemas.microsoft.com/exchange/services/2006/types"
12         xmlns:m="http://schemas.microsoft.com/exchange/services/2006/messages">
13       <m:ResponseMessages>
14         <m:SendNotificationResponseMessage ResponseClass="Success">
15           <m:ResponseCode>NoError</m:ResponseCode>
16           <m:Notification>
17             <t:SubscriptionId>hKJETtoAdi9PPWOtZDQ4MThmMDoVYB</t:SubscriptionId>
18             <t:PreviousWatermark>ygwAAAAAAAA=</t:PreviousWatermark>
19             <t:MoreEvents>false</t:MoreEvents>
20             <t:ModifiedEvent>
21               <t:Watermark>ywwAAAAAAAA=</t:Watermark>
22               <t:TimeStamp>2018-02-02T15:15:14Z</t:TimeStamp>
23               <t:FolderId Id="AAB2L089bS1kNDgxOGYwOGE5OTQ0="></t:FolderId>
24               <t:ParentFolderId Id="AAB2L089bS1kNDgxOGYwOGE="></t:ParentFolderId>
25             </t:ModifiedEvent>
26           </m:Notification>
27         </m:SendNotificationResponseMessage>
28       </m:ResponseMessages>
29     </m:SendNotification>
30   </soap:Body>
31 </soap:Envelope>
```

To acknowledge that the push notification responder has received the notification, it must reply with the following:

```
1  <?xml version="1.0"?>
2  <s:Envelope xmlns:s= "http://schemas.xmlsoap.org/soap/envelope/">
3    <s:Body>
4      <SendNotificationResult xmlns="http://schemas.microsoft.com/exchange/services/2006/
            messages">
5        <SubscriptionStatus>OK</SubscriptionStatus>
6      </SendNotificationResult>
7    </s:Body>
8  </s:Envelope>
```

To unsubscribe from receiving push notifications, clients must send an unsubscribe response in the `SubscriptionStatus` field, similar to the following:

```
1  <?xml version="1.0"?>
2  <s:Envelope xmlns:s= "http://schemas.xmlsoap.org/soap/envelope/">
3    <s:Body>
4      <SendNotificationResult xmlns="http://schemas.microsoft.com/exchange/services/2006/
           messages">
5        <SubscriptionStatus>Unsubscribe</SubscriptionStatus>
6      </SendNotificationResult>
7    </s:Body>
8  </s:Envelope>
```

To verify the health of your push notification responder, Amazon WorkMail sends a "heartbeat" (also called a `StatusEvent`). The frequency with which they are sent is determined by the `StatusFrequency` parameter provided in the initial subscription request. For example, if `StatusFrequency` equals 1, a `StatusEvent` is sent every 1 minute. This value can range between 1 and 1440 minutes. This `StatusEvent` looks like the following:

```
1  <?xml version="1.0 (http://www.w3.org/TR/REC-xml/)" encoding="utf-8"?>
2  <soap:Envelope xmlns:soap="http://schemas.xmlsoap.org/soap/envelope/">
3  <soap:Header>
4      <t:RequestServerVersion xmlns:t="http://schemas.microsoft.com/exchange/services/2006/types"
           xmlns:m="http://schemas.microsoft.com/exchange/services/2006/messages" Version="
           Exchange2010_SP2"/>
5  </soap:Header>
6  <soap:Body>
7      <m:SendNotification xmlns:t="http://schemas.microsoft.com/exchange/services/2006/types"
           xmlns:m="http://schemas.microsoft.com/exchange/services/2006/messages">
8      <m:ResponseMessages>
9          <m:SendNotificationResponseMessage ResponseClass="Success">
10             <m:ResponseCode>NoError</m:ResponseCode>
11             <m:Notification>
12                 <t:SubscriptionId>hKJETtoAdi9PPW0tZDQ4MThmMDoVYB</t:SubscriptionId>
13                 <t:PreviousWatermark>AAAAAAAAAAA=</t:PreviousWatermark>
14                 <t:MoreEvents>false</t:MoreEvents>
15                 <t:StatusEvent>
16                     <t:Watermark>AAAAAAAAAAA=</t:Watermark>
17                 </t:StatusEvent>
18             </m:Notification>
19         </m:SendNotificationResponseMessage>
20     </m:ResponseMessages>
21 </m:SendNotification>
22 </soap:Body>
23 </soap:Envelope>
```

If a client push notification responder fails to respond (with the same OK status as before), the notification is retried for a maximum of `StatusFrequency` minutes. For example, if `StatusFrequency` equals 5, and the first notification fails, it is retried for a maximum of 5 minutes with an exponential backoff between each retry. If the notification is not delivered after the retry time has expired, the subscription becomes invalidated and no new notifications are delivered. You must create a new subscription to continue to receive notifications about mailbox events. Currently, you can subscribe for a maximum of three subscriptions per mailbox.

Changing Amazon WorkMail Web Application Default Settings

You can change many of the default settings for the Amazon WorkMail web application.

To change the Amazon WorkMail web application default settings

1. In the Amazon WorkMail web application, on the menu bar, choose **Settings** (gear) icon.

2. In the navigation pane, select one of the tabs listed below to update the settings as appropriate.

3. Press the F5 key to refresh and activate the new settings.

Topics

- General Tab
- Email Tab
- Email Rules Tab
- Automatic Response Tab
- Calendar Tab

General Tab

Change password
To change your password, choose **Change password**, and then follow the instructions on the screen.
If Amazon WorkMail is integrated with your corporate directory, you might have to change your password using Microsoft Windows or corporate password management tools.

Language
To change the language in which Amazon WorkMail is displayed, select a language from the list. To change your date format and time format, select a format from the list.

Mailbox Usage
Shows the current amount of storage space used. To reduce your mailbox size you can empty the **Deleted Items** folder, delete older messages, or delete messages with large attachments from your folders.

Address Book
To select a default address book, in **Select Default Folder**, select the address book to use.
The default address book is loaded when choosing **Address book** from the main menu bar or when selecting the To/Cc/Bcc field when composing a new email.

Keyboard shortcuts
To control the Amazon WorkMail web client using your keyboard, select the **Turn keyboard shortcuts on** check box. The following shortcuts are available:
Creating new items
CTRL + SHIFT + A—New appointment
CTRL + SHIFT + B—New meeting request
CTRL + SHIFT + X—New item
CTRL + SHIFT + C—New contact
CTRL + SHIFT + D—New distribution list
CTRL + SHIFT + F—New folder
CTRL + SHIFT + M—New mail
Basic navigation
CTRL + 0...9—Switch between different contexts, such as inbox, calendar, and so on
CTRL + SHIFT + 1...9—Switch between different views
CTRL + SHIFT + ARROW KEYS Switch between tabs
ALT + S—Open shared folder/store
CTRL + SHIFT + L—Close tab
All views

F5—Refresh
CTRL + A—Select all items
CTRL + SHIFT + G—Print list
CTRL + P—Print selected item
CTRL + M—Open copy/move dialog
ENTER—Open selected item
DELETE—Delete selected item
Items
CTRL + P—Print item
CTRL + S—Save an item, such as mail, contact, and so on.
CTRL + ENTER—Send an item, such as mail, meeting request, and so on.
Mail
CTRL + SHIFT + U—Toggle read/unread
CTRL + SHIFT + H—Toggle red/complete flag
CTRL + R—Reply
CTRL + SHIFT + Y—Reply all
CTRL + F—Forward

Email Tab

Display preview pane
You can choose to view a preview of items to the right of the content pane or below the content pane. You can also choose to turn off the preview pane.
Changing the view from the mail application using the **View** menu updates this **Display preview pane** setting.

Close email when responding
When this setting is off, if you open an email in a new tab, a new tab is opened next to the existing one when you reply to the email.

Format
You can compose new mails as **Plain text** or **HTML**.

Default font
Specifies the default font used in all new email messages.

Default font size
Specifies the size of the default font.

Always request a read receipt
Select this check box to automatically request read receipts for every message you send.

Respond to read receipt
Select whether Amazon WorkMail should always send a read receipt, never send a read receipt, or whether you should be prompted before sending a read receipt.

Signatures
You can create several signatures for different purposes. For example, you can create a signature for business and one for private use, or create a long signature one for new emails and a short signature for replies and forwards. After you have created one or more signatures, you can (optionally) specify which one to use for new messages and which one to use for replies and forwards.

Email Rules Tab

You can create email rules that help you focus on important emails and keep your inbox tidy. Rules are stored on the server so that they can filter the mail before it arrives in your inbox.

You can create as many rules as you want and with each rule, you can set various conditions to trigger the rule. You can also set various follow-up actions after the rule has been triggered.

You can construct complex rules to deal with large email volumes or complex work flows.

To create a new mail rule, choose **New**, and then in the **New email rule** dialog box, define the rule.

You can set various conditions and actions that Amazon WorkMail performs on every message that meets the criteria you define.

Automatic Response Tab

The Amazon WorkMail web application lets you mark yourself "in" or "out" of the office. Specify the message that is sent automatically in reply to all incoming messages while you are away.

To prevent someone who is sending you several emails per day from getting a reply on each message, automatic responses are only sent one time to any specific email address. This also prevents a mail flood in case the person who sends you the email also has automatic responses turned on.

When **Automatic response** is enabled, and you log to the Amazon WorkMail web application, a warning message is shown to remind you that the **Automatic response** is set. The warming message prompts you to turn it off.

Calendar Tab

First day of the week
If your week starts on another day than Monday, you can set it to any other day using this setting. The calendar then always starts with this day.

First week of the year
Specify how the calendar should begin the year.

Start of workday/End of workday
Specify the part of the day that is marked as "workday." The calendar shows this time period in a slightly different color so you can easily see when an appointment or meeting is scheduled outside office hours. The default values for office hours are 8:30 - 17:30 (8:30 AM - 5:30 PM).

Calendar resolution
If your appointments frequently start at other times than each half or entire hour, or have a duration other than (multiples of) 30 minutes, then you can change this value to better fit your needs.
Setting the value to less than 30 minutes makes the Amazon WorkMail web application zoom in on the calendar, so you scroll more when you are using a smaller screen.

View multiple calendars
Specify how multiple calendars should be displayed by default in the Calendar. **Side-by-side** displays all calendars next to each other. **Overlay** displays all calendars transparently on top of each other, where each calendar has its own color.
This setting has no effect when you are only displaying one calendar.

Default reminder time
Specify how long before the start of the appointment the default reminder should occur. This setting can be overruled for any appointment by editing it manually in the calendar. The default is 15 minutes.

Default all-day appointment reminder time
Specify the reminder time that is automatically set when you create a new all-day appointment. The default is 18 hours. This setting can be overruled for any appointment by editing it manually in the calendar.

Working with Accessibility Features

You can use screen readers and keyboard shortcuts with Amazon WorkMail for easier accessibility.

Topics

- Supported Screen Readers
- Using Shortcut Keys with Amazon WorkMail
- Working with General and Email Settings
- Using the Global Address Book
- Working with Email
- Working with Folders

Supported Screen Readers

You can use the following browser-based screen readers with Amazon WorkMail:

- Firefox—NVDA
- Internet Explorer—JAWS
- Safari—VoiceOver

Note

For **NVDA/JAWS** some actions work best when you enter or exit **Forms** mode.

Most of the commands provided can be used across all screen readers. Some screen readers, such as VoiceOver, offer keyboard-based combinations for voiceover controls. For example, in VoiceOver use **VO+Right** arrow in place of the right-arrow key on your keyboard.

Note

The following exceptions apply only to VoiceOver:

VO+Spacebar replaces **Enter**. **VO+Left/Right** arrows replace **Tab** and **Shift+Tab**. **Fn+Delete** replaces **Delete**.

For best accessibility, use plain text as the email format and disable the **Preview** pane. For information, see the *Email settings* section in Working with General and Email Settings.

Using Shortcut Keys with Amazon WorkMail

Shortcut keys are globally applicable and not specific to screen reader software. Keyboard shortcuts are disabled by default. To enable keyboard shortcuts, see Working with General and Email Settings.

Note
For Mac, use **Cmd** instead of **Ctrl**.

Keyboard shortcuts for creating new items

- **Ctrl+Shift+A**—New appointment
- **Ctrl+Shift+B**—New meeting request
- **Ctrl+Shift+X**—New item
- **Ctrl+Shift+C**—New contact
- **Ctrl+Shift+D**—New distribution list
- **Ctrl+Shift+F**—New folder
- **Ctrl+Shift+M**—New message (email)

Keyboard shortcuts for basic navigation

- **Ctrl+0...9**—Switch between context such as inbox, calendar, etc.
- **Ctrl+Shift+1...9**—Switch between different views
- **Ctrl+Shift+Arrow keys**—Switch between tabs
- **Ctrl+Shift+L**—Close tab
- **Alt+S**—Open shared folder or store

Keyboard shortcuts applicable to all views

- **F5**—Refresh
- **Enter**—Open selected items
- **Delete**—Delete selected items
- **Ctrl+A**—Select all items
- **Ctrl+P**—Print selected items
- **Ctrl+M**—Open copy/move dialog
- **Alt+Shift+G**—Print list

Items

- **Ctrl+P**—Print item
- **Ctrl+S**—Save an item, such as a message, contact, etc.
- **Ctrl+Enter**—Send an item, such as a message, meeting request, etc.

Email

- **Ctrl+R**—Reply
- **Ctrl+F**—Forward
- **Alt+Shift+U**—Toggle between read/unread
- **Alt+Shift+H**—Toggle red flag/complete
- **Alt+Shift+Y**—Reply all

Working with General and Email Settings

You can modify the default and email settings in the Amazon WorkMail web application.

General Settings

The general settings have the following defaults, which can be modified.

- **Date format**—English (US)
- **Address Book**—Global Address List
- **Keyboard shortcuts**—Off

To change the default account settings

1. In the Amazon WorkMail web application, press **Tab**.

2. At the *Username* prompt, enter your username and press **Tab**.

3. At the *Password* prompt, enter your password and press **Tab**.

4. At the *Sign in* prompt, press **Enter**. The default starting point for the cursor is the **Inbox**.

5. Hold down **Shift+Tab** until the screen reader reads *Settings button*. Press **Enter**.

6. In the **Settings** screen, the default landing point is the **General** tab.

7. Press **Tab** until the screen reader reads *Date format English U.S combo-box read only*. Hold down **Alt+Down** to open the field and use the **Up/Down** arrows to select the date format.

8. Press **Enter** to confirm the selection.

9. Press **Tab** to move to the next section, which is **Mailbox Usage**. This section is read-only. Press **Tab** again to reach **Address Book**.

10. Use **Alt+Down** to open the **Select Default Folder** menu, and the **Up/Down** arrows to change the default view. Press **Enter** to accept the change.

11. Press **Tab** to move to the **Keyboard shortcuts** menu. The default setting for this is off. Press **Tab** to select the field. You can select and clear the box using the **Spacebar**.

12. Hold down **Shift+Tab** until the screen reader reads *Save changes button*. Press **Enter** to save the changes.
    Note
    Restart Amazon WorkMail to have the date format and keyboard shortcut changes take effect.

Email Settings

Email settings have the following defaults, which can be modified.

- **Display preview pane**—Right
- **Close email when responding**—On
- **Format**—HTML
- **Default font**—Narrow Sans Serif
- **Default font size**—Normal
- **Always request a read receipt**—Off
- **Incoming mail**—Ask me before sending a response

To change email settings

1. In the Amazon WorkMail web application, hold down **Shift+Tab** until the screen reader reads *Settings button*. Press **Enter**.

2. In the **Settings** screen, the default landing is the **General** tab. Press the **Down** arrow to select the **Email** tab.

3. Press **Tab** to access the **Display preview pane** field. Hold down **Alt** and use the **Up/Down** arrows to choose a display setting.

4. Press **Enter** to confirm the selection.

5. Press **Tab** to choose whether to **Close email when responding**, using the **Spacebar** to select or clear the field.

6. Press **Tab** to move to **Compose email**.

   - For **Format**, use **Alt+Down** and the **Up/Down** arrows to toggle between **HTML** and **Plain Text**. Press **Enter** to confirm the selection.
   - For **Default font**, use **Alt+Down** and the **Up/Down** arrows to scroll through the list of available fonts. Press **Enter** to confirm the selection.
   - For **Default font size**, use **Alt+Down** and the **Up/Down** arrows to choose a font display size. Press **Enter** to confirm the selection.

7. Press **Tab** to move to the **Always request a read receipt** checkbox. Press **Spacebar** to select or clear the box.

8. Press **Tab** to move to **Incoming mail** for the **Respond to read receipt** setting. The default setting is **Ask me before sending a response**.

9. Press **Tab** to move to **Signatures**. Press **Enter** to open the **New signature** composer. Compose your signature. When you're finished, hold down **Shift+Tab** until the screen reader reads *Save changes button*. Press **Enter** to save the changes.

Using the Global Address Book

You can use the Global Address Book to search for a user, change the default view, and send email to specific contacts.

Using the Global Address Book

1. In the Amazon WorkMail web application, hold down **Shift+Tab** until the screen reader reads *Address Book pop-up button*. Press **Enter**.

2. In the **Address Book** window, the default landing is the search bar.

3. Start typing in the search bar and press **Enter** to search for matching entries. You can also press **Tab** until the screen reader reads *Submit search button*. Press **Enter** to select it. To clear the search, press **Tab** until the screen reader reads *Clear search button*. Press **Enter**.

4. You can send a message to a contact with the Address Book using the **Up/Down** arrows to navigate the list and select a row. Hold down **Shift+F10** to open the context menu, and choose **Send email**.

Troubleshooting the Amazon WorkMail Web Application

Solutions to the most commonly encountered Amazon WorkMail web application errors are listed below.

Connection Loss

If you lose connection to the server due to a network error, Amazon WorkMail displays a warning message at the top of the screen. You cannot retrieve data from the server, but you can continue working with items that are currently open. In the warning message, the timeout is shown for the next time the Amazon WorkMail web application will try to connect to the server. To skip this timeout, and immediately retry, you can click the warning message. If the connection has been reestablished, the warning message is removed, and you can continue working.

Session Expired

If your session has expired on the server and you are no longer logged in to the server, Amazon WorkMail displays a warning message. You can return to the login screen, or you can keep the Amazon WorkMail web application open (without being allowed to open or save any data).

Mail cannot be saved

If your email gets stuck in your outbox and doesn't get sent, Amazon WorkMail displays this error message. This may be due to a network issue. Try saving the email again to resolve this error.

Email redirection is not working

If your email redirection is not working, you may need to update the domain sending authorization policy. A new API operation allows you to redirect email to any address, regardless of whether it's part of your domain. This needs to be done manually for domains added before October 13, 2016. For more information, see Editing Domains.

Document History

The following table describes the important changes to the Amazon WorkMail User Guide.

Change	Description	Release Date
Mailbox permissions	Various updates related to the Permissions UI.	April 9, 2018
Push notifications	With the Amazon WorkMail EWS API, you can receive push notifications about changes in your mailbox, including new email and calendar updates. For more information, see Working with Notifications.	February 7, 2018
Support for SMTP	You can configure your IMAP email client to send email through Amazon WorkMail. For more information, see Connect to Your IMAP Client Application.	May 10, 2017
Support for a wider range of email clients	You can now use Amazon WorkMail with Microsoft Outlook 2016 for Mac and IMAP email clients. For more information, see Connect Microsoft Outlook to Your Amazon WorkMail Account and Connect to Your IMAP Client Application.	January 9, 2017
Support for Amazon WorkDocs email attachments	Included guidance for attaching a file from Amazon WorkDocs and saving an email attachment to Amazon WorkDocs. For more information, see Download Attachments.	October 19, 2015
Support for Microsoft Outlook 2011 for Mac	Included guidance for using Microsoft Outlook 2011 for Mac with Amazon WorkMail.	August 18, 2015
Preview Release	The preview release of Amazon WorkMail.	January 28, 2015